NORTHGATE LIBRARY

JUL -- 2017

D0820966

NO LONGER PROPERTY OF
SEATTLE PUBLIC LIBRARY

*Also*
*by*
*Maureen N.*
*McLane*

**Same Life**
**World Enough**
**My Poets**
**This Blue**
**Mz N: the serial**

# Some Say

# Mau–reen N. McLane

Farrar Straus Giroux : New York

# Some
# Say

Farrar, Straus and Giroux
18 West 18th Street, New York 10011

Copyright © 2017 by Maureen N. McLane
All rights reserved
Printed in the United States of America
First edition, 2017

Library of Congress Cataloging-in-Publication Data
Names: McLane, Maureen N., author.
Title: Some say : poems / Maureen N. McLane.
Description: First edition. | New York : Farrar, Straus and
    Giroux, 2017.
Identifiers: LCCN 2016045043 | ISBN 9780374266585 (hardback) |
    ISBN 9780374714802 (e-book)
Subjects: BISAC: POETRY / American / General.
Classification: LCC PS3613.C5687 A6 2017 | DDC 811/.6—dc23
LC record available at https://lccn.loc.gov/2016045043

Designed by Quemadura

Our books may be purchased in bulk for promotional,
educational, or business use. Please contact your local
bookseller or the Macmillan Corporate and Premium Sales
Department at 1-800-221-7945, extension 5442, or by
e-mail at MacmillanSpecialMarkets@macmillan.com.

www.fsgbooks.com
www.twitter.com/fsgbooks
www.facebook.com/fsgbooks

10 9 8 7 6 5 4 3 2 1

not a symbol
but a sample
a living piece
the mortal sun

# Contents

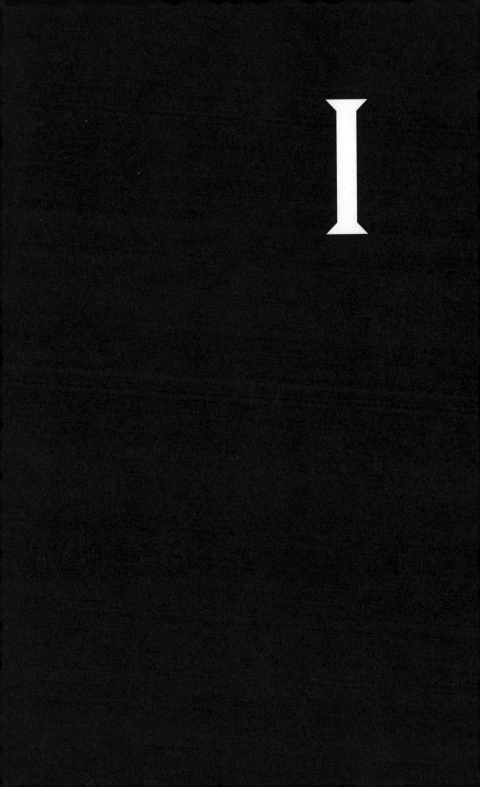

I

# As I was saying, the sun

& the moon and all stars
you can name
are fantastic!

It's not cool
to be enthusiastic
not chill

to say hey!
There's a fucking sun
still shining

over every goddam thing
except what happens at night!
—& even when we don't see it

3

it's there the sun
like god
but more palpable

less responsible
though both burn.
A turning world

is flat
until mountains
and valleys and axes

tilt the models
men make. If I say abstract

I don't mean ideal
I mean real.
The lids of our eyes

are fewer than cats'.
Watch it bear down on us
brute beautiful fact

and what stuns
is a sun stuck in the sky
by no one.

## OK Let's Go

Let's go to Dawn School
and learn again to begin

oh something different
from repetition

Let's go to the morning
and watch the sun smudge

every bankrupt idea
of nature "you can't write about

anymore" said my friend
the photographer "except

as science"
Let's enroll ourselves

in the school of the sky
where knowing

how to know

and unknow is everything


we'll come to know

under what they once thought


was the dome of the world

# Mesh

Everything in the world
has a name
if you know it.
You know that.

The fungus
secreting itself
from the bark
is Colt's Hoof.

The dignity
of cataloguers
bows before code.

The thing
about elements—
they don't want
to be split

Every time
I collide with your mind
I give off—
something happens—
we don't know what

Particles, articles
this bit, a bit
digital, simple
fission, fusion
—a great vowel shift.

I saw the world
dissolve in waves
the trees as one
with the sun
and their shadows.

The trees on the shore
The trees in the pond
branch in the mind

The screech of the subway
decelerating its knife
into the brain
of all riders

8

In the morning the hummingbird
In the evening five deer

Why should I feel bad
about beauty?

The postmodernists
are all rational
& sad though they mug

in zany gear.
Everyone knows
what is happening
They disagree why
& what then.

It turns out
the world was made for us
to mesh.

## Some Say

Some say a host
of horsemen, a horizon
of ships under sail
is most beautiful &
some say a mountain
embraced by the clouds &
some say the badass
booty-shakin' shorties
in the club are most
beautiful and some say
the truth is most
beautiful dutifully singing
what beauty might
sound under stars
of a day. I say
what they say
is sometimes
what I say
Her legs long

and bare shining
on the bed the hair
the small tuft
the brown languor
of a long line
of sunlit skin I say
whatever you say
I'm saying is beautiful
& whither truth beauty
and whither whither
in the weather of an old day
suckerpunched by a spiral
of Arctic air blown
into vast florets of ice
binding the Great Lakes
into a single cracked sheet
the airplanes fly
unassuming over    O they eat
and eat the steel mouths
and burn what the earth
spun eons to form
Some say calamity
and some catastrophe
is beautiful    Some say
porn                Some jolie laide

11

Some say beauty
is hanging there at a dank bar
with pretty and sublime
those sad bitches left behind
by the horsemen

# Forest

There you go
walking in the woods
as usual
ignoring the trees . . .

The fifteen kinds
of trees
you refuse
to lodge in your skull.

Here's the stand
of Norway spruce
mostly dead.
Someone's bad idea.

13

We are going
to monetize
everything
so value shines
clear as the sun.

Just because,
things happen

Just because
things happened
doesn't absolve
whoever's alive

The future's
a lure
& hungry fish bite.
Curious.

You want
a solid Lutheran hymn
to praise the given
under the sign of salvation.

God an organ
few now know
how to play.

Diapason,
Aeoline Celeste—
So many stops

to make the sound
of what used to be
the greatest machine

He knew all the names
and if he appeared
to the forest people
he appeared as a rainbow bird
on the supreme tree

There you go
making images
because you don't know the names.

## Taking a Walk in the Woods After Having Taken a Walk in the Woods with You

Now I cannot not see
the blight everywhere

# Prospect

Thus should have been our life

sexual, untaxable . . .

And the tyranny of thumbs

and hips and skulls

which brought us down from the trees

and condemned us to permanent screens

was a regime no declaration

could free us from.

You are too young

to think so much

about death she sd

the older woman

who dressed in her

long-trained dancer's muscles

did not seem old

as we are made to see them

residual forgettable a little shameful

but one must not hurt them lest

the fragile carapace under which

we live ramshackled days
shatter, as if in a thought experiment
of a world without oxygen for five seconds
become a world in free fall
all untreated metals
spontaneously welding together
& our every cell exploding
in a hydrogen collapse.
Melancholia is realism
and realisms are isms and
the thing itself retreats
into the forest now there &
there calling the first new bird
in spring unheard
for four long months
What was a month to the men
with only a moon & a sun

§

Once upon a time
when everyone had pubic hair
and read books and had been taught
penmanship and bombs
and oh good PB&J there was pleasure

in things specifically now
forgotten or rather abandoned
Let's forsake the crusted nostalgia
of the global ruling classes
Go fist yourself
a roasted duck on a warm spit

§

Let us be decorative and unafraid
Let us approach the line at the edge of a margin of a bay
& love the asymptotic whatever
Let us salute the clouds even when they shit on us
as if the earth were an excrement of some sky
and we still saluted it
Let all the centuries collapse
into endless columns of clouds
we the survivors look on

# II

# As I was saying, the sun

is my enemy
One must not take it personally

It burns the skin
years later the surgeon
cuts off

O lidocaine
muted pain

O the women in childbirth
the soldiers     amputations
without ether

How argue
against progress
given this

In the mind's eye
the scar that skirts
the eye and dents the head

's a medal
worn for all those
once in pain now dead

# Notationals / Songs of a Season III

a gull with a shattered wing
ended the spring

∞

a day without rain
I'd almost forgotten
the shape of the sun

∞

today's reckoning
one wasp freed & one wasp dead
I am justice, blind

25

∞

it is only recently humans think
death final

∞

Julys stack in the mind
forty-five summers
become one summer

∞

I think of you
"all the time"
I don't say I "grieve"

∞

same orchard
same grasses
same bicycle
you'll never ride

∞

why not say
I think of you more
now you're dead

∞

was it hysteria
or simply being awake

∞

to be calm and still
as the Morandi bottles
on the windowsill

∞

If I wait long enough
the hummingbird

∞

this life a work-around
death

∞

your hands on my face
if you were a blind woman
you'd feel the new lines

∞

I guess I'll have to live
with this my face

∞

bright morning sun through the slats
but the sun in my head is dead

∞

yesterday's neurosis
looks judicious
this morning

∞

dream of a clear sky
in a clear pond
the mist on the lawn
unchemicaled

∞

it's not that I expect to touch
the sky with my two hands

∞

after a storm
even you must concede
the birds again sing

# As I was saying, the sun

is a thin thing
in a thin spring

this late fall day
won't know.

Yellow gingko
leaves on sidewalks

slip December
nearer. I see

that death
growing in you

as I never
before saw

anything new.
Another one

brought to the horror-
show to shock

herself into
the real.

It's not
the moral thing

that appalls
but the thinking

I don't mind
no mind

for it's minding
that blanks

the world

# Hinge

november's embers
leaves in the eaves
forestall all
winter inters
wind in
white height
snowing knowing
burial a real
thing hinge
creaking kings
onward wards
children run
regal eagle's
flight light
over hover
there here
leaf if
forever ever
beckons kin

| | |
|---|---|
| home's | own |
| storm | horn |
| ending | *ding* |
| *an sich* | such |
| things | sing |
| seasons | on |

## Mount Mansfield

The stream is frozen
except what's flowing
below what's frozen.

It will be snowing
on the bare mountain
long before what's frozen
resumes flowing.

At the first sign of spring
my long-lost cousin
will go to man the fire tower
on the clear mountain.

No cattle lowing
but fat sheep penned
in a hill crofting
for a short season

as if nothing were ever frozen
every path always open
& someone stood guard
in every season.

## Crux / Fern Park

In the otherwise untroubled snow
I saw where I'd turned around

faint gashes the trace in the snow
of the way my mind ran aground

on the question of which way to go
There was no way to know the direction

from a thinning sun
no way to follow the hum

of snowmobiles to a possible road
The way I stood was pressed in the snow

the first ski marks almost effaced
by a second and then a third guess

distressing the snow with poles
and the old lust to move

even at 5° below
and only a chickadee

and a black unidentifiable thing
out of the corner of the eye

running through the woods
clearly knew their own going

No roads diverged
no ski trail split

the mind forked itself
and doubled back

and back and back
among the black spruce and tamaracks

# Peony

There's a woman
walks through me
sits at the table
reading Rumi
You are in your body
as a plant is in the earth
yet you are yes the wind
and she is bending
into the wind her death
and she is a thin tree
and what she never saw
this peony

# Man in Field

The man who walked out
of his body walked out
into a field he once mowed
avidly, crazily, with a headlamp
at night because grasses
are for mowing or not, and wood
for stacking, and a meadow
for springing into flowers
an orange cat can sniff and browse
for years after the man walks out
into the field as ash on the field
becomes the field

# Fell for a Friend

fell, *n.*

1. *Chiefly British.* An upland stretch of open country; a moor.
2. A barren or stony hill.

—*American Heritage Dictionary*

Night fell.
Fall fell.
Fiends Fell.
Fare you well friend.

# You Would Have Liked It

You would have liked it
the moss-sunk trail
and sunshafts bolting the woods
open. You would have.

## Tips for Survival

In the Arctic wear only 100% wool.
Sleep in snow caves not tents.

Take a pole on a glacier.
It will help if a crevasse.

In polar bear country sleep in the center
of the ring your dogs make.
The bear will be less hungry when.

Don't date flyboys.
Carry blister tape.

Antibiotics. Antibiotics.

If a giraffe is staring at anything
but you, run.

Make eye contact
on the subway
only if.

Always have three plans.

Don't fuck people
who don't read.

Accept no gift
unless you want that relationship.

Need it. That ship will carry you.
There will never be enough time

or later. Now now now now now.

III

# Dawn School

I'm going to go
to Dawn School

to learn how the day
cuts itself

out of the night
that shelters

all sleepers
and wakers

I'm going to remember
the sun

in a blank cave
this our world

said the fabulous
sunstruck philosopher

who after all returned

# Meanwhile

while I slept
the pears bloomed

while I slept
the cherries

while we slept
forsythias

while we slept
crocuses

while we slept
snowdrops

while we slept
hyacinths

while we slept
we slept

## For You

It's been a long while since I was up before you
but here I am, up before you.

I see you sleeping now that I am up before you.
I see the whole morning before you.

How dare the sun be up before you
when the moon last night promised to hold off the sun
   just for you!

I hear the church bells ring before you.
Most days it's true the birds are up before you.

I should make the coffee, as I am up before you.
I might just lie here though before you

wake up. Let me look at you, since I am here before you.
I am so rarely simply quiet before you.

The orange cat who'll soon wake you is always up
  before you.
In Morocco or Lamu the muezzin would be up before
  you.

And yes it's true most days the sun is up before you—
long before me and a while before you.

Shall I make it a habit to be up before you?
To see your soft cheek and feel your breath if I am up
  before you?

Shall I prepare the mise-en-scène for you?
Hold the shot of the sun in my eye just for you?

Go back to sleep my love for you
are only dreaming I am up before you.

# Girls in Bed

You are in bed
and Antigone's dead

once again though offstage
and alive on the previous page

doomed proud girl
elective fatalist

& the dark Doñas
and perved-out girls

are facing off
at the Met

Velázquez
vs. Balthus

and you know who
wins. A sleeping

woman is an erotic
thing in many a painting

and Albertine sleeps
away it seems

a million days
as Proust swerves

ever unto a swerving
desire. But/And

you are sleeping
and no one's painting

or writing or looking
You're sleeping by the cat

in another room
and Sinatra croons a tune

"as charming as hell even yet"
on NPR. Where we are

isn't fixed by any GPS
or pinpointed location

can't be mapped by street name
city state or nation

O the drift as between
America and Europe

as between girls
in bed and girls dead

The vast Atlantic
suddenly reveals

itself a thin
watery thing covering

a continental shelf
An Atlantean upsurge

cracks the abyssal plain
proves what looks sundered

is so deep under linked

# Mariner

I saw your albatross
today in the sun
a hallucination
above Lake Champlain.

The flickering silver
resolved into gulls
a mile off, the flashing quiver
unremarkable birds.

There on the ocean
the sun outshone the sun
& the Pacific
became the horizon.

Albatrosses are common
in that region
the horse latitudes
you long ago left
& I'm sailing into

the stars above say
when I ask them to speak
in a simple human way
which is to say my way

or the highway . . . rebarbative
Milky Way I will not be here
long nor stay to drink
from the sky's cup no matter how long
my eyes decline to blink.

# Note to Self (Strandhill)

Freshwater woman—
time to remember the taste of the sea.

## Rauschen

could you tell the rush of the trees
from the rush of the sea

# Notationals / Songs of a Season IV

another cry
which of your four calls
o loon

∞

little puffs of cloud
a summer sky—
I'm here I'm here!

∞

Cottonelle . . .
sky brought to you by . . .

∞

I swam far out but not so far
I couldn't hear the thunder

I swam far out but not so far
I ever forgot where you were

∞

clouds eat a red moon
it's gone
it was orange
you have to trust me

∞

I didn't fall into the cold lake
and thus I am alive
and not even cold
thank you gone god

# Confession

Even if I had plenty to do
I would still look at clouds.

Every day the sky organizes itself
as if for watchers.

In the storm the deer pauses, legs charged.
Then he resumes eating grass.

In the boathouse we talk of love
or sex or getting laid.

There are so many things to confide.
Today I am keeping faith with the sky.

## Enough

The storm dissolved
into sun.
We had no expectation.

The clouds full
of pomp ignored
whatever

the wind did
below. It was enough
to flow or float

or clouden
a clouded sky.
A robin flew by

the scratch
of a baby red squirrel.
We told ourselves

we would read

nothing for six weeks.

The world was full

as it always was

of wings of meaning & nothing.

## Party Dress

I am still the girl
who wants a new dress
for the party
The party
in my honor
which will be memorable
only if the dress shines
like Helen's face

# White Dress

It is not too late to wear a white dress my love though
  the fall
suspends itself in the trees
whose leaves shine a green wind that will not pass
until it passes this day the boat you pick up and lift
off the pond it too ripples
& the duck skitters to a landing
all the world a sudden field
to land in     Why dive
when one can glide in a white dress
well-groomed feathers the ruffled pond
will fit in your pocketbook
your pocketbook will fit
in the knapsack where all the tools
of the visible are labeled
and ready—we know how to fix everything
today, the sky its cirrus and the grass
browning without rain without
rain nothing grows but the mind
its bones unbending

It is not too late to wear your sandals love though we live
far from the desert the desert is here its sands in the
    soles
of your sandals the desert is the shifting plain
we've not yet visited and the Tuareg
have yet to climb the White Mountains
It is not too late love to know everyone
& everything shines a weird light the pantheists
call soul the fortunetellers aura or something
the realists scoff at oh the sad scoffers and mickey
    mockers
Is it too late to buy them a drink

Is it too late to wear a delicate necklace
fashioned by a Greek artist you've never met
Too late to say hey what was all that fuss
about the asteroid Too late to buy the burial plot
And is it too early to say some days it seems just Wow
you look so elegant there unadorned in a white dress
& sandals at the perfect juncture of the season
and life oh do not bend your head any further lest the
    stalk break
the flower of the now

# Balsam

And to think
that only now I begin
to feel it

A long walk
required to know
the ground

The sap of the balsam
we burst from the blisters
on the bark still sticks

I could not
not touch it

the bark
your neck

# Notationals / Songs of a Season V

three deer under the apple tree
luxe, calme et volupté

∞

how a body goes
vibrating in a white dress
what a body knows

∞

fireworking your way—
shoot star shoot!

∞

red-eyed vireo
preaching to the cedars
no conversions

∞

fat bee in the bloom
polyamorous bee
polyfloral honey
sweet to think
it's all designed

# Song

I don't mind
admitting the daylilies
catch my eye
and sing to me
July July

I don't mind
traveling to see
a famous garden
in a friend's book

I don't mind
remembering the fungus
on a blighted beech

I don't mind
the moss invading my mind
so soft & wet this nook

# IV

# Black Bird

The gabble in the night
you said must be turkeys—

after the babble
of the sweating city

what to make
of the rhodomontade

of the bullfrog?
The peepers

outshriek the club kids.
The metallic

screech of the grate
cranked upward

by the guy at the newsstand—
morning orison

crossed by a single crow.

## Coyotes

OK you heard the coyotes
and I didn't.

It is always this—
you this, I that

and a canyon
opening between.

Five short yips
and then the known long howl.

You can hear
the highway even here.

## Seal Cock

When you said
seal cock
I heard seal talk.

Frozen stiff
four dozen packed in a box
in the ice-cream meat truck
in the Arctic.

Open the box:
it was inarguable
what they were.
You tossed them
to the dogs

who loved them.
A vegan here
you concede

you'd eat meat
& white bread all year
up north.

No way
not to eat what you have to
and live if not like it.

## The relativity

of pests:
how I felt
about you
fifty minutes into
a call that while
not deeply annoying
was truly boring
The deer that first appeared
a dark mass
against a distant tree
resolved into a beauty
of dun fawn
the long-tuned elegance
of an ancient body
now riddled with ticks
O there are too many
& we must cull
we will shoot humanely
what's excessively

about to wipe

us or our friends

out but let's wait

on killing

sentiment

gets its moment

here before the gun

the archaic click

of a phone back on the hook

# What Can I Help You With?

Is it my phone
Is it my camera
talking to me—
The trees talked to Dorothy

or no they reached out
to grab her for killing.
My phone's gone dead
What's in my head

is placeable
like a church
on a map.
I've got a map app

for my head
in your lap.
A blowjob app
to guide us

through the last lap.
Home coming.
There's no place
like home.

Rhyme's a snap.
The gates shut clean
on McMansions
where porn's on the screen

and *sur la table*.
Remember when
sounds aligning
meant the sun

was shining
on birds singing,
bells chiming?
Me neither.

Oh but I do.
They taught me
to hear them
those old dead ones

who are only dead
as old stars
still illuming
alternate planets

where everyone alive
worships a sun
whether or not it's dead
or a dying one

# Nirvana

the perfect transparency
of my beautifully
lived life available
to all with free
wi-fi and a working currency
the goddess of exchange
the goddess justice
they are weighing
the immaterial
there are no more souls
to balance and damn
no heaven to acquit
no purgatory to rectify
debt and I have derived
myself from my parents
and all I took
unwitting in
my skin "alive
with mouths"

I fed for years
on bad air and lotions
modern potions
for capturing
what I wanted
o slave o me
self-traded along the oceans
of *I want I want*
but not to desire
is to die
or to reach
enlightenment
as the eastern
as they used to call them
sages said

# Update

what threatened all day
is here—thunder, rain,
and now your text

## Upstate

If only the storm
would decide the day
I could breathe.

New corn in the pot
An apple on the desk—

The small towns
of upstate New York
list to one side.

The centuries
were male. Trees
drooped. Lightning
restored the electricity.
Let's Go Team.

# Folk School

I am going to Folk School
to learn how to be
one of my people.

Dogsledders, that is.
Paragliders.
Eaters of carrots

and hamburgers.
We are going to map
the genome

of my people
which is an excellent people
its every pupil

earning a gold star
for human being
in a cosmos full
of people and black holes.

Look there are my people
on the rim of disaster!
They're frozen forever
while elsewhere
the work of living goes on
in a space-time continuum
the ages haven't yet broken.
My people humble people
who expect nothing.

# Reunion

They were all there
every member
of the family.

No one cried.
No adult.
The children shrieked

and cried and called out
in the usual ratios.

Cousins are fun
as first crushes.

Everything I know
about sex I learned
from my first cousin

my dead ex-father-in-law
told his son.
Fathers transmit things

overtly and not.
They obsess their sons
the more they are remote.

Some devour their children
Some say Well Done!

After the great feast
the band of brothers
congratulates itself.

There is only one killing
they need do.
After that comes a world

of exchanges and reunions
a need for nametags and potato salad.
The dead gods laugh

in old print.
They cannot believe
how it turned out.

# Real Time

How that old flow
became a thing marked
by a factory bell.

The morning beer
put aside for capital.

To be or not to be
said Alexander Graham Bell
to an emperor down the line.

Mary Had a Little Lamb
& Edison grooved his foil.

There are so many things
to remember and telephone.

In the morning the Pledge of Allegiance,
at noon the Angelus.

It was terrible
to lose ritual.

Some people
float better in a sea
of continuous partial attention.

I know a man
gets jazzed by his smartphone.
It is his mind

& everything he knows
& everyone.

A world of many ringtones
one *La Marseillaise*.

# Headphones

The French Revolution vanishes
into rain.

The café where Camille Desmoulins
jumped atop the table and roared
is closed.

So too the one grocery store
in the Adirondack town.

Three years fade
into centuries of raised voices.

When I think "of my childhood"
what am I thinking?

Spiro Agnew's widow died.
Everything a function
of stochastic patterns
this rain also obeys.

Can't you hear it
the unpitched wave soaking
the spruce?

Can't you hear them screaming?
Morton Feldman said
pointing below the Berlin pavement stones.

One deafens to live
till you're deafened to all.

I'm canceling all the noise
my earthened ears bring me.

## One Canoe

Recalcitrant elephants
begin to attack.
The angry young males
of murdered mothers

Any Martian could see it
how we did it

The historian of the future
is amazed. So much feeling

once in so many bodies.
*But maybe they were different
didn't think or feel that much.*

95

Apocalypse is easy
Thinking's hard

Should we summon
a Roman Stoic to narrate?
Someone secretly thrilled
by the gore?

The clouds move through
an Adirondack sky unscored
by satellite towers.

People want what they want
& what they want is never one thing.

All that desire
sliming a space rock.

Shivering the air
a loon's cry.
There is only so much
you can care for or carry

& for this there is
no one canoe

V

# Rowing

A small decision
the wind could tip

whether to row
east or west

with the wind
or against

as if the wind
were constant

& at any moment
wouldn't shift

as if rowing
were what you were doing

you adrift

## Come Again / Woods

They party in the woods
as if they were meant for pleasure
not timber.

Cuts heal.
Second growth.

As if this world
were made for us.
Some think so.

"People piss me off
specifically and species-wise."

Oh well.

The beer bottle
on the abandoned foundation
of a cabin. Civilization.

Mangy teenagers
acid rain and a sunset.
Who's done with "nature"?

That old sun
just now
blew me away.

## Yo

I am so demanding
I expect the humming-

bird to appear
at the anointed hour!

And you pioneer
birch, you there

with your carpet
of leaves the forest resents—

I salute you
I no swinger

of birches or men . . .
Paper, yellow, white

what are you
thin and perfect

on the lawn?
The spotted fawn

noses below
your waving leaves

and autumn
is welcome

so folded
into a summer so long

we cannot imagine
your limbs bare.

Talking to birches
I am an idiot

& I know you get it
reader—no idiolect

this dialect
riddled with defects

time will fix
or forget. Whatevs.

It is never not time
to say hello
or goodbye.

# Aversion

First I flushed out the turkeys
then I startled the bird

with the white patch
on its back singeing

the trees. Nothing
did not flee.

Forest judgment
against the species

in me.

## Rabbits

American rabbits don't give birth
in holes but in dens
unlike Europeans. Who knew.

Rabbits are born blind
with no fur. Hares
are ready to go, furred
with eyes open.

If I wait here long enough
all the true things
will disclose themselves.

# Trail

Just like you
to take a surveyor's tag
for a trail marker . . .

Hello!
Welcome
to property!

Time for a prospect
poem that will encompass
all I & my rich friends

survey. Americans.
Democratic vistas.
Whole swaths

of your country
are a third-world country
sd the German

recycling the trash.
And upstate: Time
to get your teeth pulled.
A new set's cheaper.

There's an algorithm
for all this
which is no solace.

Bandage the mind
with an old tune
& new words.

# Meditation After Berlin

Could a lake
make your mind?
New York potholes blare
a lack of care.

Kids are kids—
sculptural, feral.
Some of them
one likes, like flowers.

On a morning with a light wind
and the sun spangling the lake
everything is given
and eternal.

The dirges are over
and no one remembers why
they were invented.

They'll be back
those old songs
& the heavy tread on the dirt.
The kids die
later or sooner

Some are lucky
& some take their chance.
The end of couples dance
& romance.

The GDR barred
youth culture.
A dream of a permanent
socialist waltz
seasoned by foxtrot.
Everyone wanted Levis
on their asses in the Trabis
they all knew how to fix.

Everywhere people are tender
& mistaken and some
are evil.

To make
no more things
but songs
anyone could sing.
To tune precisely
every string
and go without fear
of the simple or complex thing.

# On Not Being Elizabethan

How did they do it
shape their complex minds
into chiming lines
of woe & sorrow
crowning frowning
every rhyme sieved in time
to a bell they all heard ringing
Singing no more singing
but stinging an enemy
into his own dole and song
decrying everything
the enemy said
as the enemy's wrong
When the mind's a ready surface
the stamp's impress will take
What is it to suffer
the mood of a queen
It seems ridiculous
a sudden kiss

a glance or gesture
a vow a letter
derailing a life
unto a dungeon tower
An insurrection every hour
it seems I suffer
Can she excuse my wrongs
with virtue's cloak?
Can I compose this song
of air and ancient smoke?
The fires still burn
Dead hearts still yearn
A tiny repertoire
of end rhymes enough
to win a queen an empire
enough to set a cold heart afire
enough to make an English lute
a Greek lyre
enough to make the killing block
a singing pyre

## Music Theory / Tuning

The sky was the mood.

Children looked freshly.

It was important

not to tell them

yet about slavery.

Someone would.

Maybe I should.

History hurt me

into identity

& then a motet

clothed me new.

There was no way

to be without

a body & live.

Some songs accuse

Some forgive

Some just go

# R&B

The old songs teach you to cry
and when.
The new ones are pumping
your blood to the sky.

More moans than cries.
A blue note is waving
itself into a melisma.

So much feeling
spun out of flesh
into air.

The lobes in the throat
are the globe in the club
in your mind.

Late style nearly obscures
the god hidden in a tabernacle

beseeched by the seeker
for joy.

So much obligatory crying
and everything wrong
in this song.

# Fairway Loop

I didn't strip the bark from the birch
though I wished to.

Though it pinched and itched
I didn't scratch the bite.

Without any saddle
I mounted the horse
who knew the way home

This body my horse
This horse my body
We made every turn
as one together

The mind flits
a butterfly     then rests
on a steady spine

a spine we've long
been stretching to round
every bend ahead.

# Notationals / Songs of a Season VI

oak lichen carpet
glacial erratic
porcupines shit here

∞

all the way up
what you thought
was the smell of apples
was cedar

∞

maples skimmed . . .
an orange brush
hello frost

∞

to be able to say
*thus*
today's yes

# Against the Promise of a View

A difficult climb
to a beautiful view—
I don't like it.
I don't like the way
you make me go
positively Protestant
all this deferral
up to a future
only you've seen
the ascent always leveraged
against an alien payoff
already prescripted.
When we get there
I'll be dead
tired too tired to view
the view the way
I wanted. I wanted
the way to be beautiful
as a stroll in the Hanging

Gardens of Babylon
or the wisteria-laden
lanes of the rose garden
in the Bois de Boulogne
as beautiful as a jammed
Sixth Avenue crosswalk
in midtown. I wanted
to be going nowhere
nowhere we know
not to have to breathe
so hard into a future
someone else promised.
I know
reputable studies show
the capacity
to delay
gratification
makes for a happy
person & nation
but oh
I just want
& want now
a perpetual
beautiful stroll
nowhere

I don't want
to look back
& say ah
that was so
worth it
because even
if it was
it wasn't.
I don't want
to keep my head down
for miles alert
for insurgent roots
a falling branch
my legs punctured
by stinging flies
that harry the way
only to be able to say
at some notional
top however beautiful
*how beautiful*
*—& see, no insects here*
*& why not lunch—*
Somehow
it was just
the glorious sun

and twelve islands
inlaid in a lake
& the distant silent
powerboats
Somehow it was a vision
of all as dust
If I go
on pilgrimage
I want every age
to be a stage
one can look around
and say how interesting
& yes a cup of coffee
would be nice
I'm not going anywhere
fast but where
we're all going

# Night Sky

Spackled black
the pure uncertain light
invites you to climb
a ladder on a clear night
to a vanished point

Messages arriving
the messengers long dead
& the airplanes traversing the stars
in their flight are carrying
the future dead

Metal wombs
for earthly angels
sleeping in rationed seats
The trays don't easily fold back up
now that dinner service is complete

The baggage is checked
stored above and below

The attendants provide
blanket and pillow

All day and night the sky alive
with wanderers
who nonetheless know
where they are going
because the ticket says so

and in a long look
a still point moves slow
across a climacteric
you hadn't thought to trace
or to that satellite
to give a specific national face

The man in the moon
is the hare making rice cakes
in Japan & the stars long ago
swallowed the Greeks

They look back at us dumb
in their old religion
The belt of Orion encircles
no man's hips

and Cassandra is crying out
through foregone lips

A crab crawls and fish swim
in unscannable seas
The sky drinks
in its black miseries

A comfort to sailors
who take two seamarks
One mark will never suffice
in the unmarked dark

When an unseen hand
or death metal band
crumples the sky
in untellable folds

see the North Star kiss Mars
& Venus unveil her face
as admen brand the stars
and men sell shares in space
the multiverse contracts
to a single implacable place
where nothing you can imagine
will never not take place

## Envoi: Eclipse

I don't trust myself
not to look

# Acknowledgments

I am grateful to the editors, publishers, and staffs of the publications where some of these poems first appeared, sometimes in different form: The Academy of American Poets "Poem-a-Day" series; *Blackbox Manifold*; *Eborakon*; *Granta*; *The Nation*; *The New Republic*; *The New Yorker*; *Painted, Spoken*; *The Paris Review*; *Plume*; *Poetry*; *Poetry Daily*; *Psychology Tomorrow*; *Shearsman Magazine*; *The Spectator*; *Tin House*; *T Magazine: The New York Times Style Magazine*.

"Note to Self (Strandhill)" and "One Canoe" appeared in *Parallels*, a feuilleton edited by Alice Lyons, Curator/Poetry Now 2015, for the Mountains to Sea Book Festival, Dun Laoghaire, Ireland. "Night Sky" first appeared in a chapbook, *New Year* (ed. Will Vincent, 2014), accompanying the screening of Adam Shecter's video *New Year* (2014) at 11R Gallery (NYC). "For You" has been set to music by the composer Judah Adashi. It was first performed by Caroline Shaw (voice) and Caleb Burhans (viola). All thanks to these artists, poets, musicians, and editors.

For their care with and attention to this book, thanks as well to Jeff Clark (again!), Carolina Baizan, Maureen Klier, and Sarah Scire.

For support during the writing of this project, deepest thanks to Blue Mountain Center, the Corporation of Yaddo, The MacDowell Colony, and the New York University Global Research Initiative. I am grateful to these institutions and the provisional communities and enduring friendships they sponsored.

And to those who asked or answered: Rachael Allen, Diane Boller, Matthew Campbell, David Caplan, John Clegg, William Corbett, Kelvin Corcoran, Valerie Cotter, Robyn Creswell, Alex Dimitrov, Jeff Dolven, Adam Fitzgerald, Dai George, Eileen Gillooly, Saskia Hamilton, Langdon Hammer, Cathy Park Hong, Alex Houen, Sarah Howe, Valentina Ilardi, Paul Keegan, Cheston Knapp, Danny Lawless, Brantly Martin, Ange Mlinko, Paul Muldoon, Matt Neff, Luke Neima, Karl O'Hanlon, Meghan O'Rourke, Tony Perez, Adam Piette, Richard Price, Justin Quinn, Vidyan Ravinthiran, Don Selby, Don Share, Dinos Siotis, Ersi Sotiropoulos, Lorin Stein, Jack Thacker, and, especially, all thanks to Jonathan Galassi.

A grateful salute as well to Harriet Barlow, Blair Braverman, Emily Drury, Barbara Ess, Dylan Gauthier, Sabine Heinlein, Bruce King, August Kleinzahler, Timothy Morton, Anahid Nersessian, Tom Pickard, Karen Russell, Carole Slatkin, Ben Strader, and Kendra Sullivan: whose thoughts, work, and comments diversely vibrate here.

In memoriam Daniel Aaron; Shahab Ahmed; Richard Brick; Julia Targ.

As I was saying: this is for Laura.